Riddles
From a
Recluse

Wallace Pustinjak

Preface

To experience these riddles as they are meant to be, it is necessary to set aside all preconceived notions of custom, identity, and truth. For by their very nature, riddles renounce the limitations of other forms of expression in order to reach their own plane of abstract complexity. Though heavily influenced by the deceitful nature of puzzles, riddles embody the elegant wordplay and extensive wit of poetry. Taking aspects of frustration and delight in equal parts, they combine to form a potent mélange of the most bittersweet variety. In order to solve a challenging riddle, one must endure a gauntlet of emotions encompassing far more than mere curiosity or bemusement. First, there is a sense of disbelief. *How could such seemingly disparate and meaningless hints ever coalesce into a single answer?* Next, frustration tends to take over. *I've thought of everything I can and nothing makes sense. What am I missing?* It is at this point in the process that the reader has a choice of which path to take: capitulation or perseverance. If capitulation, then the same scenario will repeat itself without end: a few feeble attempts to ascertain any sort of meaning, a grudging admittance of the difficulty, and then a guilty peek at the end of the book for the answer. I myself have acted in a similar manner, and I know firsthand that the path of least resistance offers very little satisfaction. If perseverance trumps despondency, however, then I can guarantee that the answer will be uncovered eventually. It may take days, weeks, months, or longer, but I see this duration as of little consequence. I am of the opinion that time becomes irrelevant in the pursuit of one's goals, and it is to this tenet that I hope you will adhere. Rather than running through a mental checklist of objects and ideas until you stumble upon a solution that satisfies every stipulation, I suggest a more holistic and passive approach to reaching the correct conclusion. Do not simply seek to pull the answer from thin air in an instant, as this is not the way riddles are meant to be treated. Instead, go about your life with a mind open to metaphor and insight. Remove the blinders of boredom and complacency, for they numb your ability to uncover authentic meaning in each moment that passes by. Open your eyes to the minutia of everyday life and fully experience the covert grandeur of existence. For what is a riddle, if not an invitation to live life with joy and awe?

To anyone who asks questions

while seeking personal truth.

Never accept complacency

or mistake the beliefs of others for your own.

Riddles

A golden disc, held high by all.

That in the end must always fall.

In constant motion it appears,

To nullify our deepest fears.

This bringer of horror, dread, and fright,

Is robbed of us in the dark of night.

Bringer of wonder and joy so gay,

Its powers are known throughout the day.

Uncountable army below the trees,

Bringing the mightiest men to their knees.

Their ranks fill the land when weather is fair,

Yet under a roof, dominion is rare.

Ideal refuge from the sun.

A foe that you cannot outrun.

Distorted mirror, ever near.

The catalyst of primal fear.

Truly with a breadth astounding.

After twilight ever hounding.

Bone breaker and finger taker,

Deceptive safety past the shore.

Sharp as a knife, snubbing out life,

Along the roof and on the floor.

Four regal champions, unrelenting.

Bearing garments of green, gold, red, and white.

Charging ever forward, unrepenting.

An army of days, a legion of nights.

Born of the cold and born of the heat.

Pacing the world on legs oh so fleet.

Swiftest up high, lethargic down low.

The actions are seen, the form does not show.

Remnants of a fallen empire,

Burning with a hidden light.

Buried under the snow of fire,

Seedlings of potential might.

Emerald fingers lay a ruby floor,

Grasping upward forevermore.

Yet all through life they strive toward,

The unattainable sapphire hoard.

The longer you evade my grasp, the closer I will be.

For those enslaved by illness, I come to set them free

There are those who cheat me, but none will defeat me.

For those who do seek me, they will soon meet me,

But few are those who willingly greet me.

A heavy load will hasten my arrival,

In sustenance I find a bitter rival.

After dusk falls I will conquer completely,

Yet following dawn I still whisper sweetly.

Rugged of old, yet no longer so bold.

Freed from the grasp of the ice and the cold.

Our prowess is humbled, our walls have been tumbled,

Our once mighty citadels have all now crumbled.

For now we lay low as a steady earthen flow,

Yet our gradual demise was far beyond slow.

The gift of a fine steed, from a well established breed.

A virtue sought by those who may have apparent need.

Yet if you force an early bloom,

Then it may prove to be your doom.

For an artist in a rush is an utter fool indeed,

When quality is sacrificed in favor of this creed.

A blanket that brings cold,

And smoothes a rugged face.

Swift wind does make it bold,

And tears the pristine lace.

I am a blade, ever cutting deeper.

I am an engine that could fuel the world.

I am a slave, the ocean my keeper.

I am a tree with sleek branches unfurled.

A brittle, white, and sheathless spear,

Ever brandished and bringing fear.

Though another goes by the same name,

An utterly foreign claim to fame.

Far greater range, yet of the same size,

Singing the song of a foe's demise.

A bound serpent dances on the cave floor.

Writhing guardsman of the windy door.

Sharp yet supple and mute yet speaking.

Devoid of hunger, nourishment seeking.

I turn the grass to silver, the earth below to steel.

My teeth are nonexistent, though my bite is real.

A shining sea of diamonds, engulfs the world by night.

Yet as the day progresses, is vanquished by the light.

With twelve eggs on order, the cook sat and thought.

"One at a time if I like it or not."

With three in the freezer and three in the pot,

Three in each hand neither too cold nor hot.

The first two were airy, or so he remembers,

The last two both burnt up and ended in embers.

My shriveled hibernation is shattered by a scream.

Scalding rejuvenation restores my youthful frame.

My black blood gushes outward, as in a horrid dream.

And though the act seems wicked, it soothes the one to blame.

Do you know me? I think you do.

For if not then you would be through.

My highly sought companionship,

Brings gifts of anesthesia,

Paralysis, a loss of sight,

And most often amnesia.

And though these gifts may seem most vile,

Do not take them for granted.

For if you will forsake this friend,

Your coffin shall be planted.

Unlike other rulers I am strengthened by neglect.

Over my jurisdiction, great taxes I elect.

When routine dues are paid, I am weakened severely.

Yet if too long delayed, it may cost you quite dearly.

My vault is of the flesh, my tellers silver and bone.

The upkeep of the kingdom is financed with a loan.

At times I am a silken sheet, at times a wall of lead.

I can at once be both the curtain and the fountain head.

The raven's wing, the spider's web, I use each guise in turn.

And joyously I am bejeweled as I begin to burn.

I am the mirror image, the one who dwells beneath.

My tapered blades bite keenly, into an earthen sheath.

I pillage from a darkened land where death and mold are rife,

Yet I aim not to dole out death but rather gather life.

A pallid visage in plain sight revealed by its foe.

It does not fast, it does not feast, and yet does shrink and grow.

Much grander and yet more minute than those it stands beside.

Unendingly stalking around, a circuitous stride.

Short lived and insubstantial, though swift beyond compare.

In sharp illumination it leaps forth from the dark lair.

For those caught within its reach I say to you, "Beware!"

For deadly potency is masked by beauty gold and fair.

A patchwork quilt of shifting cloth, no pattern stays for long.

Some think it bright and others bleak yet neither view is wrong.

For those under the distant edge find evidence of wear,

A multitude of threadbare gaps that dawn will mend with care.

A golden treasure, pilfered from gems, each a discrete vault.

The keepers of the wealth, however, welcome the assault.

For if they seek to be enriched then this price they must pay:

To see the brigands share their loot and then hoard it away.

A river running in the dark that can be hot or cold.

No creature may reside within yet life it does uphold.

A thousand streams unsuitable to quench the smallest thirst.

Instead they return to the spring from which they came at first.

An infant buried without grief and drowned with good intent.

Fallen or torn from parents' hands with no need to repent.

Rejoice as it is placed into what seems an early tomb,

That gradually is revealed as a second womb.

A throat that has no lungs, my breath can suffocate.

And from my headless mouth, shadows proliferate.

Elongated and rigid, with no blood to hold.

The role I play is vital, often in the cold.

The universal guide and competitor to pride.

An ever present confidant from whom you cannot hide.

Divergence from this law is an insidious flaw,

For those who adhere ceaselessly will surely garner awe.

I am the suitor's gaudy coat, created for flirtation.

I am the hunter's somber cloak, concealing his location.

A garment for the courier removed from occupation.

At one time drowned within the well to combat separation.

Coal encircled by a gem upon a hill of snow.

Day will burn the coal away, while night will let it grow.

Together they are priceless though alone they have no worth.

Their miniscule proportions could encompass all the earth.

Fragility disturbed and calamity unchained.

Roaring incarnation of stark grandeur unrestrained.

A stampede without legs, yet numbing implications.

Quite prone to fall away, from lofty inclinations.

Though looked upon directly I am most useful unseen.

My face determined by each side I am the in between.

A border closed to all except the immigrants of light.

Once I fall prey to injury my teeth can sharply bite.

Severed arms with piercing fur, brought forth in celebration.

Talisman with potent form conductive to rotation.

Each limb will grasp upon the next until none stand apart.

Embodiment of gaiety yet hollow at the heart.

An exodus with pounding might, the bane of desolation.

These pilgrims of the false twilight in vertical migration.

Though they carry no possessions, useful blessings they impart.

Born as one they die together, yet in life will fall apart.

Said to be contagious, an infection of the mind.

No cure is sought, no treatment bought, no pathogens to find.

Bolstered through suppression, power drained in quarantine.

Contorted face, leaving no trace, of countenance pristine.

The sound of death, the song of time.

It has no breath, yet voice sublime.

The deepest moan, the sharpest squeak.

From somber tone to joyous shriek.

Held above the temple and yet sacred in no way.

Antiquated herald for the start of each new day.

A fortress all enrobed in scales, each may have a horn.

Clinging to the spear-tip tower from which it was born.

A name given by habitation followed by the shape.

Holding offspring captive who are destined to escape.

Pillar of the roofless palace, crumbled by a breeze.

Vagrant in a boundless kingdom, phantom of the trees.

Darkness from illumination, shadow born of light.

Utilized in preservation, murderous delight.

Left behind yet never taken, set down in a row.

Seldom seen in isolation, captured by the snow.

Set apart by haste, though immobile all the same.

When left un-defaced, a betrayal of the game.

A paintless brush with sweeping strokes, the artist always near.

A rudder to the vessel that no man could hope to steer.

A metronome whose cadence is dictated by the heart.

A whip for those who have no hate or cruelty to impart.

Ceaseless blur or rigid banner varying by host.

On the smallest scale less substantial than a ghost.

Commonplace yet pivotal to rise above it all.

As a pair they triumph yet once separated fall.

As a bear sat dozing in the shade he saw a hive.

At the sight of honey his desire came alive.

Nestled in the farthest tree, an image of the sun.

Glorious beyond compare yet much too far to run.

Transfixed by the majesty he deemed it worth a shot.

From that very moment it became his only thought.

Dazzled by the future each new day soon passed him by.

As it came no closer he began to wonder why.

"Despite my fortitude and wit my life remains the same.

My goal is still so far away and who is there to blame?

I dally here and am content to yearn for that fine day,

When I shall muster all my strength and venture far away.

As I dream beneath the stars I pledge to launch my attack.

Yet in the morning ask myself what tool it is I lack?"

A signature recorded and yet never set in ink.

Illegible unless collected through the proper link.

Faded by prolific use yet magnified in wrath.

Transported directly while adhering to no path.

Inadequate reflection of each facet of the mind.

The essence of profundity once skillfully combined.

Great stairs within a tower granting never ending sight,

Or petals on a flower with no purpose save delight.

These jagged stones thrown wantonly in ignorance and hate,

Are only given substance through the change they may create.

Under certain stipulations only one will do.

While in other situations countless may be true.

Shrouded by complexity and careless oversight.

Yet upon discovery each rouse is brought to light.

The destination of each journey in the most pure form.

The sunset to a lengthy day, the rainbow to a storm.

Reciprocal component that is paired to each inception.

Revealed under hindsight as the birth of new direction.

Answers

1. The Sun
2. Sight
3. Grass
4. Shadows
5. Ice
6. Seasons
7. Wind
8. Coals
9. Trees
10. Death
11. Fatigue
12. Hills
13. Speed
14. Snow
15. A River
16. A Horn
17. The Tongue
18. Frost
19. Months
20. Tea
21. Sleep
22. Hunger
23. Clouds
24. Roots
25. The Moon
26. Lightning
27. The Sky
28. Pollination
29. Blood
30. A Seed
31. A Chimney
32. The Conscience
33. Feathers
34. The Eyes
35. An Avalanche
36. A Window
37. A Wreath
38. Raindrops
39. Laughter
40. A Bell
41. A Pinecone
42. Smoke
43. Footprints
44. A Tail
45. Wings
46. Motivation
47. A Voice
48. Words
49. Answers
50. The End

www.ingramcontent.com/pod-product-compliance
Lightning Source LLC
Chambersburg PA
CBHW031633040426
42452CB00007B/815